HORSE
POWER

SPARKY'S STEM GUIDE TO

TANKS

BY KIRSTY HOLMES

KidHaven
PUBLISHING

Published in 2023 by **KidHaven Publishing, an Imprint of Greenhaven Publishing, LLC**
29 East 21st Street
New York, NY 10010

Edited by: Emilie Dufresne
Designed by: Danielle Rippengill

Cataloging-in-Publication Data

Names: Holmes, Kirsty.
Title: Sparky's STEM guide to tanks / Kirsty Holmes.
Description: New York : KidHaven Publishing, 2023. |
Series: Horse power | Includes glossary and index.
Identifiers: ISBN 9781534540378 (pbk.) | ISBN 9781534540392 (library bound) | ISBN 9781534540385 (6 pack) | ISBN 9781534540408 (ebook)
Subjects: LCSH: Tanks (Military science)--Juvenile literature.
Classification: LCC UG446.5 H635 2023 |
DDC 623.74'752--dc23

Printed in the United States of America

CPSIA compliance information: Batch #CSKH23: For further information contact Greenhaven Publishing LLC, New York, New York at 1-844-317-7404.

Please visit our website, www.greenhavenpublishing.com. For a free color catalog of all our high-quality books, call toll free 1-844-317-7404 or fax 1-844-317-7405.

IMAGE CREDITS

All images are courtesy of Shutterstock.com, unless otherwise specified. With thanks to Getty Images, Thinkstock Photo and iStockphoto. Cover – NotionPic, A–R–T, logika600, BiterBig, Sapann Design, Sira Anamwong, KostyaTimofeev. Sparky – NotionPic, Sapann Design, Sira Anamwong. Peggy – NotionPic, Sira Anamwong. Grid – BiterBig. Driving School – Elegant Solution. 2 – KostyaTimofeev. 5 – Mascha Tace. 6 – Murad_Mammadov. 6 & 7 – KostyaTimofeev. 7 – Roman Panfilov, Borodatch. 8 & 9 – Murad_Mammadov, KostyaTimofeev. 10 – Icon Craft Studio, Mike McDonald, M-vector, hvostik, OksanaOO, Elchin Jafarli. 11 – alekseiveprev, Murad_Mammadov. 12 & 13 – Milagli. 14 – KostyaTimofeev. 15 – Murad_Mammadov, Francois Poirier. 16 – Mascha Tace. 17 – Murad_Mammadov. 18 – BigAlBaloo. 19 – ONYXprj. 20 – Mascha Tace. 21 – ArtMalivanov, DRogatnev. 22 – Francois Poirier, Icon Craft Studio. 23 – Murad_Mammadov, brown32.

CONTENTS

WORDS THAT LOOK LIKE this CAN BE FOUND IN THE GLOSSARY ON PAGE 24.

WELCOME TO DRIVING SCHOOL!

Atten-TION! I'm Jeremy Sparkplug, world-famous tank commander. You can call me Sparky. At ease, **recruits** – this is the Horses for Courses School of Motoring!

Today, you will be learning about some mean, green driving machines – tanks! So listen up, recruits. If you pass your tank test, you'll earn your Golden Horseshoe.

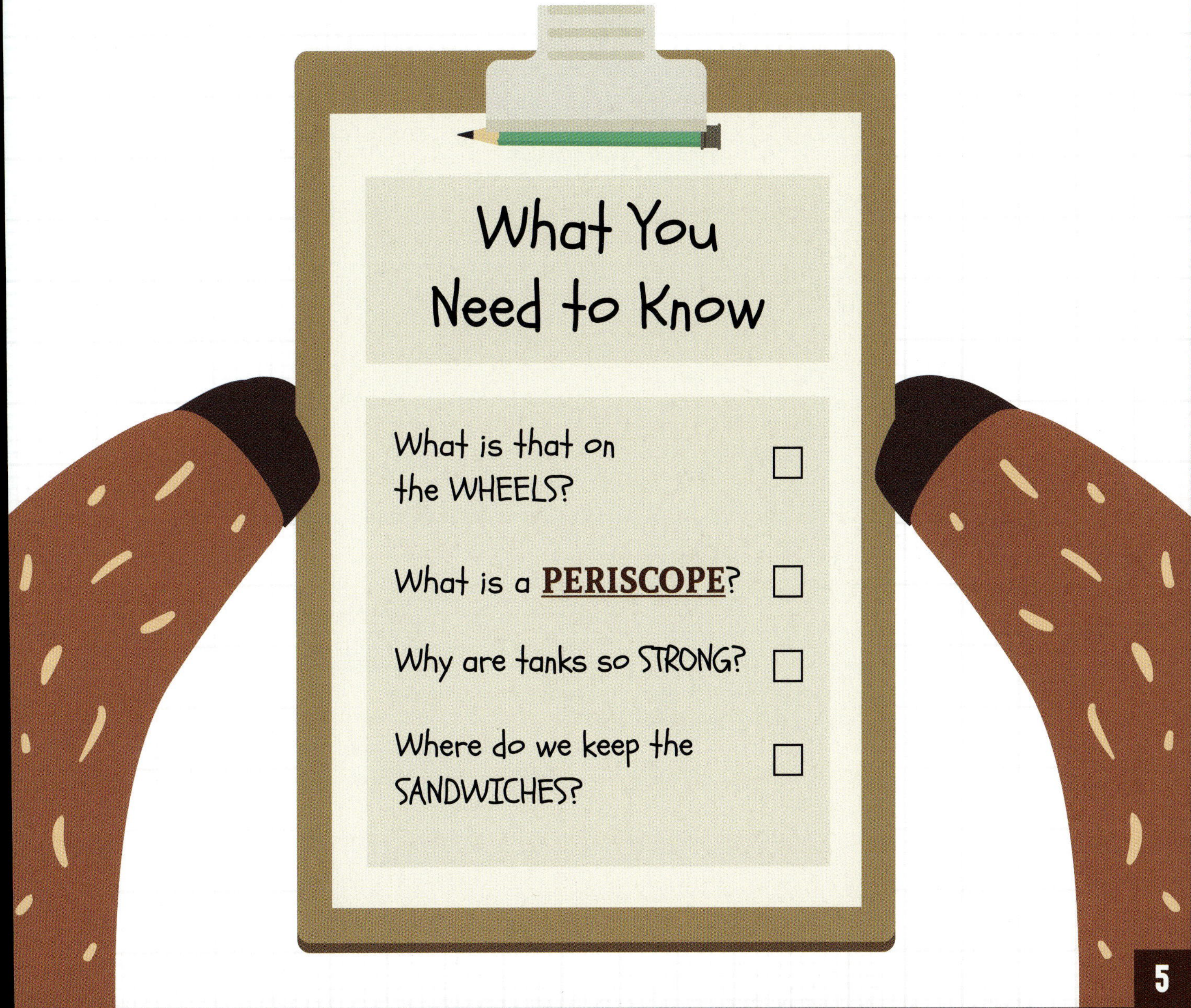

LESSON 1: WHAT IS A TANK?

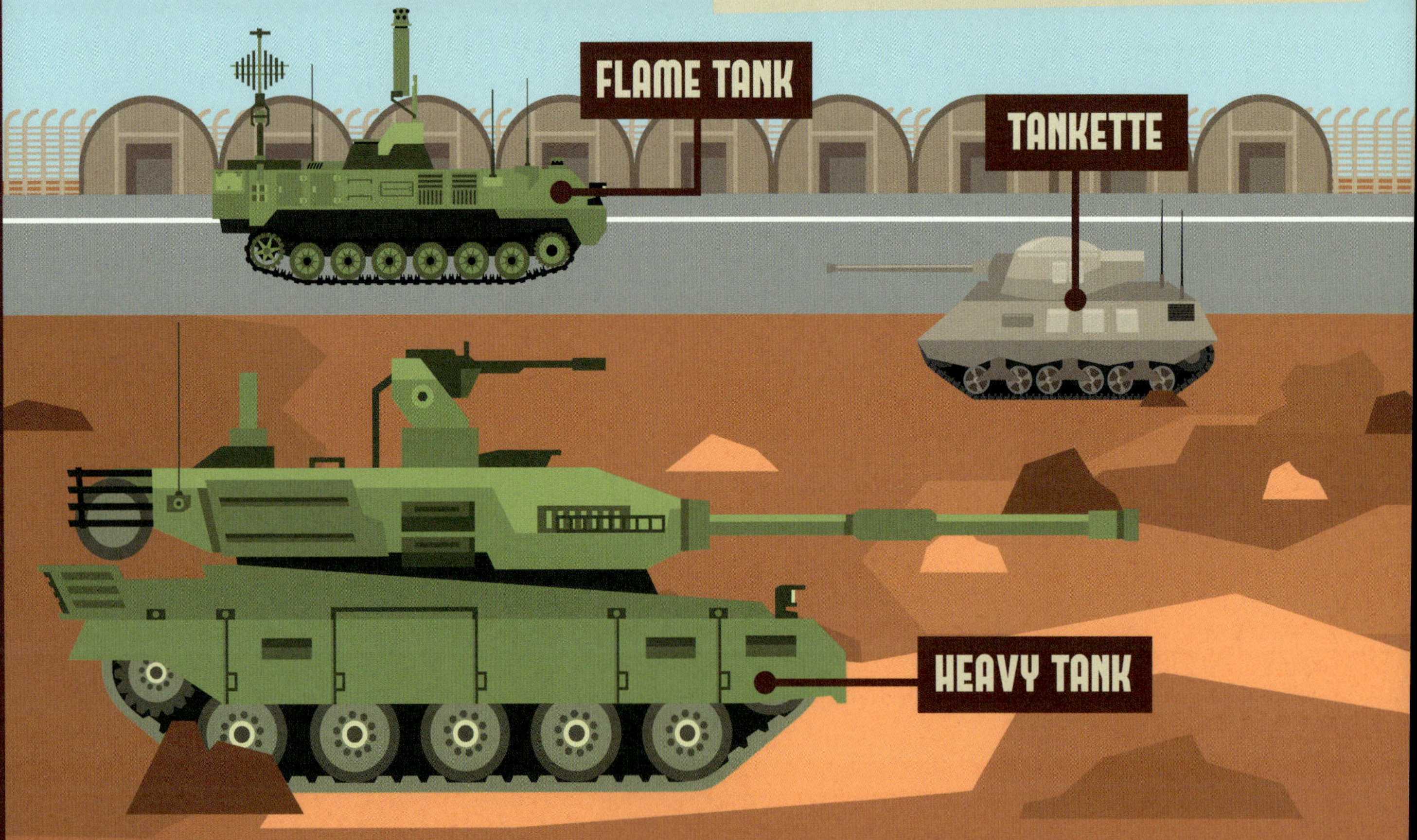

A tank is a **vehicle** used by the army. Tanks carry soldiers and weapons. They are used to protect soldiers and for attacking. They will usually have a heavy cannon and a few machine guns.

HORSES FOR COURSES
SCHOOL
EARN YOUR HORSESHOES
LIGHT TANK
MEDIUM TANK
This is Peggy. She can swing a turret with the best of them!

LESSON 2: PARTS OF A TANK

TURRET

This is where the tank's guns are. It has heavy armor.

ENGINE

Tanks have to have powerful engines because they are so heavy.

TANKS ARE ALL DIFFERENT, BUT WILL HAVE THESE SAME BASIC PARTS.

HATCH

An armored hatch on the top of the tank lets soldiers get in and out.

CANNON

This is the biggest gun on a tank.

HULL

The outside of the tank has heavy armor to protect it.

CATERPILLAR TRACKS

The wheels are inside these metal tracks. This means the wheels have something stable to drive on and don't get stuck in the mud.

LESSON 3:

INSIDE A TANK

It’s too small inside a tank to show you around, so Peggy has taken everything out and put it here so you can have a look.

SIGHTS

These are for aiming the guns.

STEERING CONTROLS

Tanks turn by speeding up or slowing down one side of the tank. This is controlled using sticks and pedals.

PERISCOPE

Periscopes help the crew look around outside.

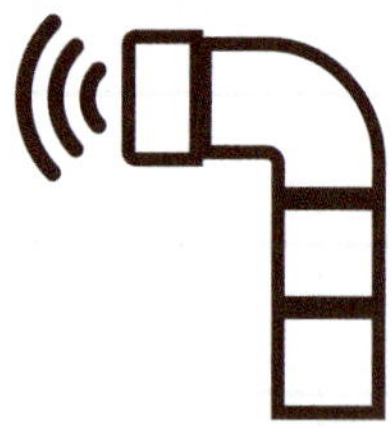

RADIO

People outside the tank tell the driver where to go.

FAN

Keeps you cool!

AMMUNITION

The bullets and **shells** are all stored in the tank.

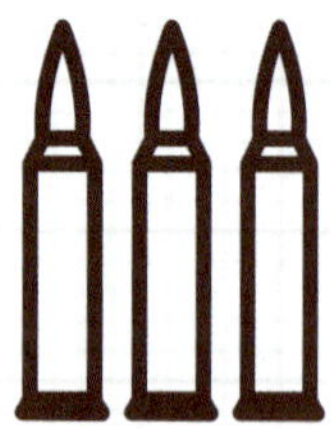

Don’t worry! These tanks are not **on duty** at the moment. There’s no ammunition inside them today.

LESSON 4:
CATERPILLAR TRACKS!

Tanks have to cross all kinds of **terrain**, such as sandy deserts, thick mud, or ice and snow. Normal wheels would get stuck, or wouldn't be able to grip. Tank wheels are wrapped in a strip of metal plates, like this:

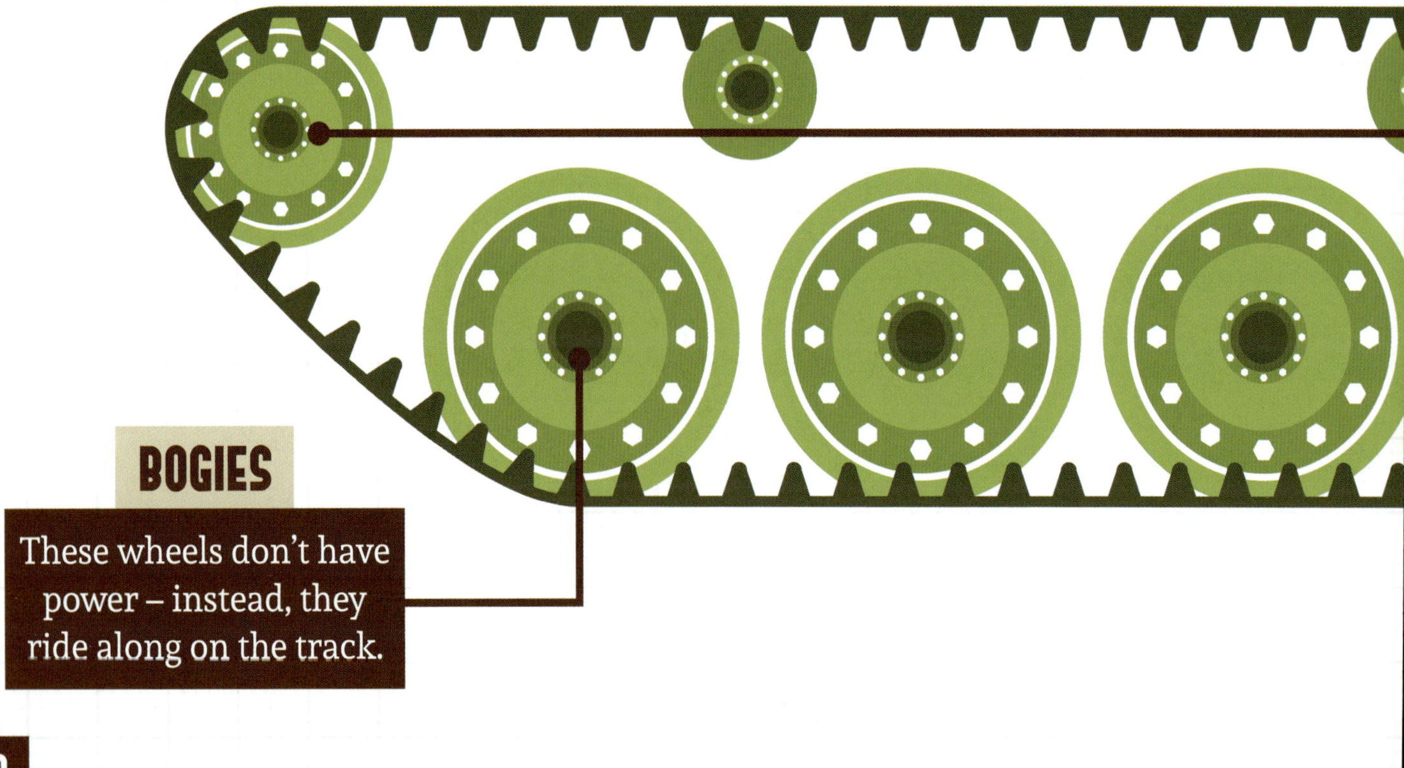

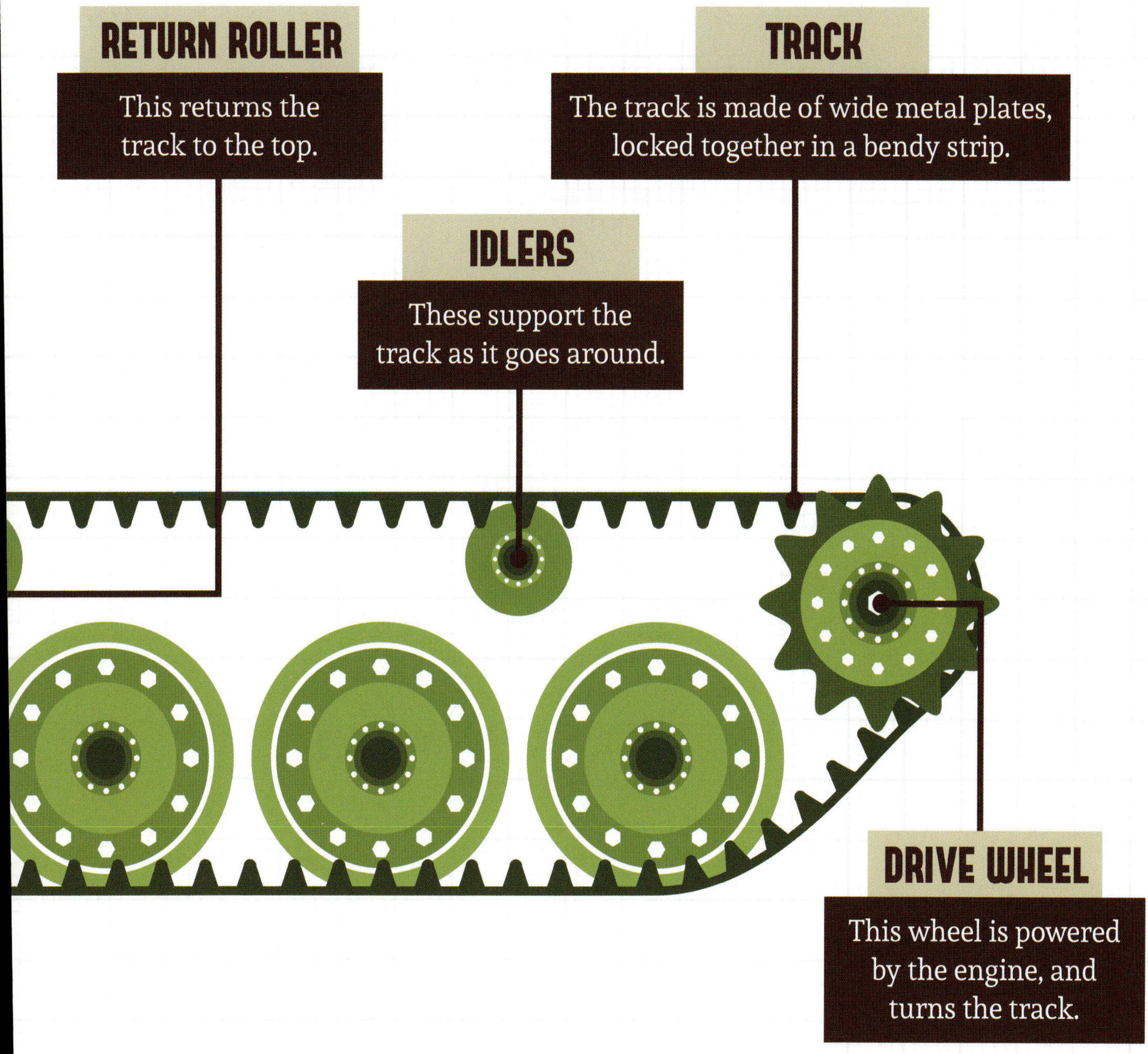
RETURN ROLLER
This returns the track to the top.
TRACK
The track is made of wide metal plates, locked together in a bendy strip.
IDLERS
These support the track as it goes around.
DRIVE WHEEL
This wheel is powered by the engine, and turns the track.

LESSON 5:

THE TURRET

The wheels and hull of a tank support the most important part – the turret. The tank's weapons are usually on the turret.

The tank commander sits inside the turret. Sometimes the gunner will be in there too. The commander's job is to tell the crew what to do, where to go, and when the gunner should...

Lesson 6: What's in A Name?

Why are tanks called, well, tanks? During World War I, the first tanks were built and had to be kept secret. To do this, the British government pretended they were building **portable** water tanks. The name just stuck!

Many types of tank have names. Tanks might be named after a famous person, such as the Churchill Mark VI. It was named after the British prime minister during World War II, Winston Churchill.

Lesson 7:

TIP-TOP TANKS

MARK I FOSTER TANK

Made during World War I, this was one of the first tanks invented. Men used them to hide behind, and they were large enough to cross over deep trenches and squash enemy **barbed wire**.

PIGEONS

During the world wars, many tanks had holes in them for releasing pigeons! These trained pigeons could take messages back to the base asking for rescue.

A PIGEON CALLED WILLIAM OF ORANGE CARRIED A MESSAGE OVER 250 MILES (400 KM) AND SAVED 2,000 SOLDIERS!

DRIVING TEST

Hooray! Time for your tank test. Will you be able to hit all these questions on target? (Check your answers on page 21!)

Questions

1. What creatures are tank tracks named after?

2. What are sights for?

3. Where does the tank commander sit?

4. What did the British government pretend they were building to keep the tanks secret?

5. How far did William of Orange fly with his distress message?

Did you get all the answers right?

Of course you did – here is your Golden Horseshoe.
You are now a Top Tank Commander, just like Peggy and me!

1. Caterpillars 2. Aiming the guns 3. In the turret 4. Portable water tanks 5. Over 250 miles!

Bonus Lesson:

CANNONBALL!

Guns in position? Check.
Gunner ready? (Peggy, that's you.) Check! Cannon loaded? Check!
Time for... SPARKY CANNONBALL!

STEP ONE

Ready...

STEP TWO

Take aim...

STEP THREE

Fire!

STEP FOUR

Look for a soft landing!

GLOSSARY

BARBED WIRE a wire with barbs or spikes that is used to keep animals or people out of a certain place

ON DUTY ready and available (military)

PERISCOPE a tube that uses mirrors at each end to see things over an obstacle

PORTABLE something that can be moved around easily

RECRUITS new members of a group or organization, such as the army, navy, or air force

SHELLS types of metal ammunition that sometimes explode

TERRAIN a type of land or ground

VEHICLE a machine used for carrying or transporting things or people

INDEX